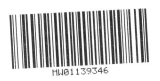

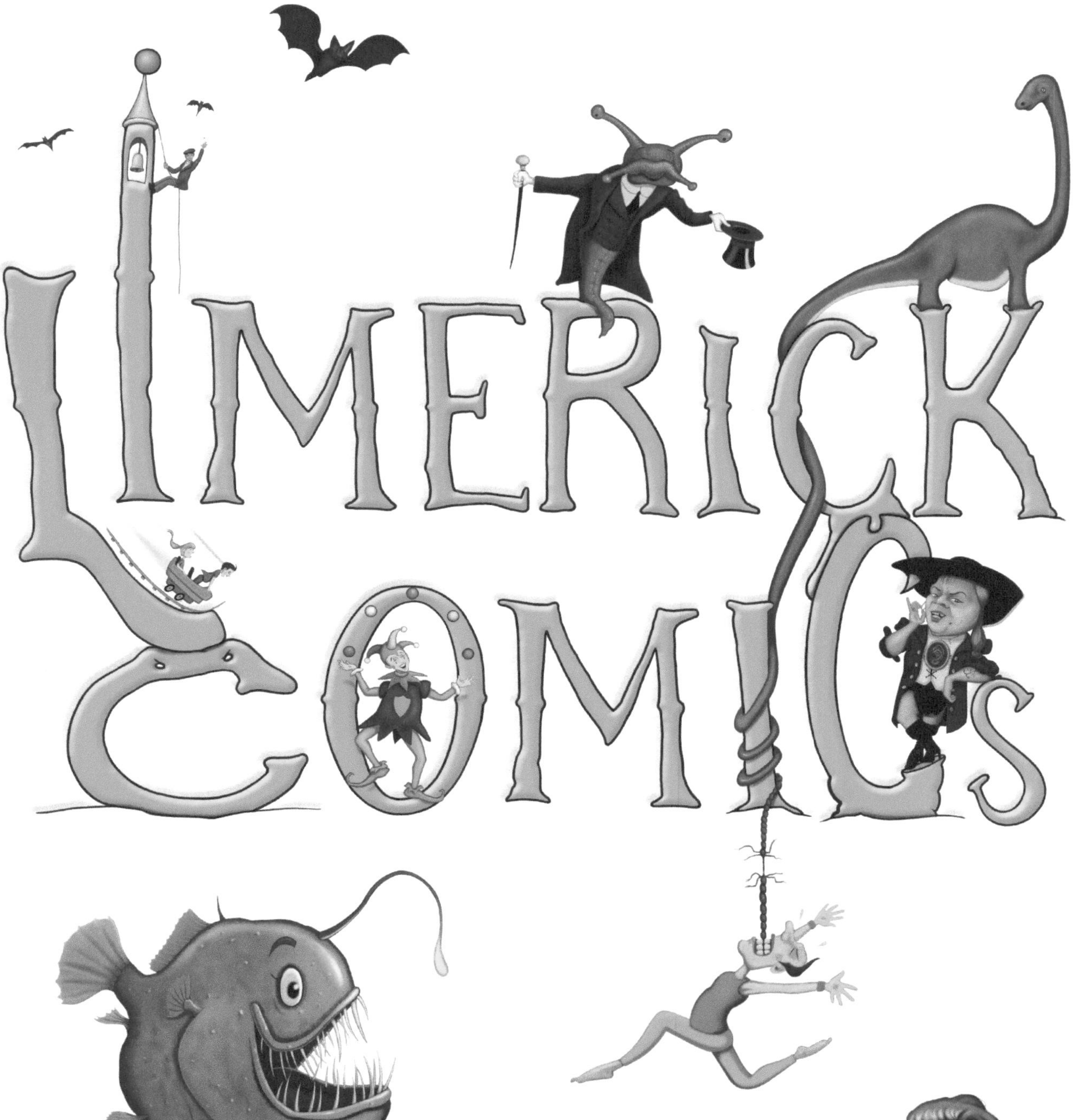

WRITTEN BY ROBERT HOYMAN

ILLUSTRATED BY STEVE FELDMAN

For Camden

Limerick Comics

Pony Express Publications

Library of Congress Control Number: 2018967243

www.LimerickComics.com
www.SteveFeldman.com

ISBN: 978-1-7328186-0-6 (hardcover)
ISBN: 978-1-7328186-1-3 (softcover)
ISBN: 978-1-7328186-2-0 (eBook)

Printed in PRC

During the Middle Ages a jester, or professional clown, was employed to amuse and entertain the King or nobleman. Being a one-man entertainer was challenging work. The jester, often referred to as a fool, played musical instruments, sang, juggled, danced, executed acrobatics, and performed puppetry. He also had to tell jokes and tactfully tease the King without being offensive. The jester's work was valued because when he brought the King to laughter it was thought to be good for digestion. Exile was a punishment imposed by an authority for a forbidden offense where a person was forced the leave the country.

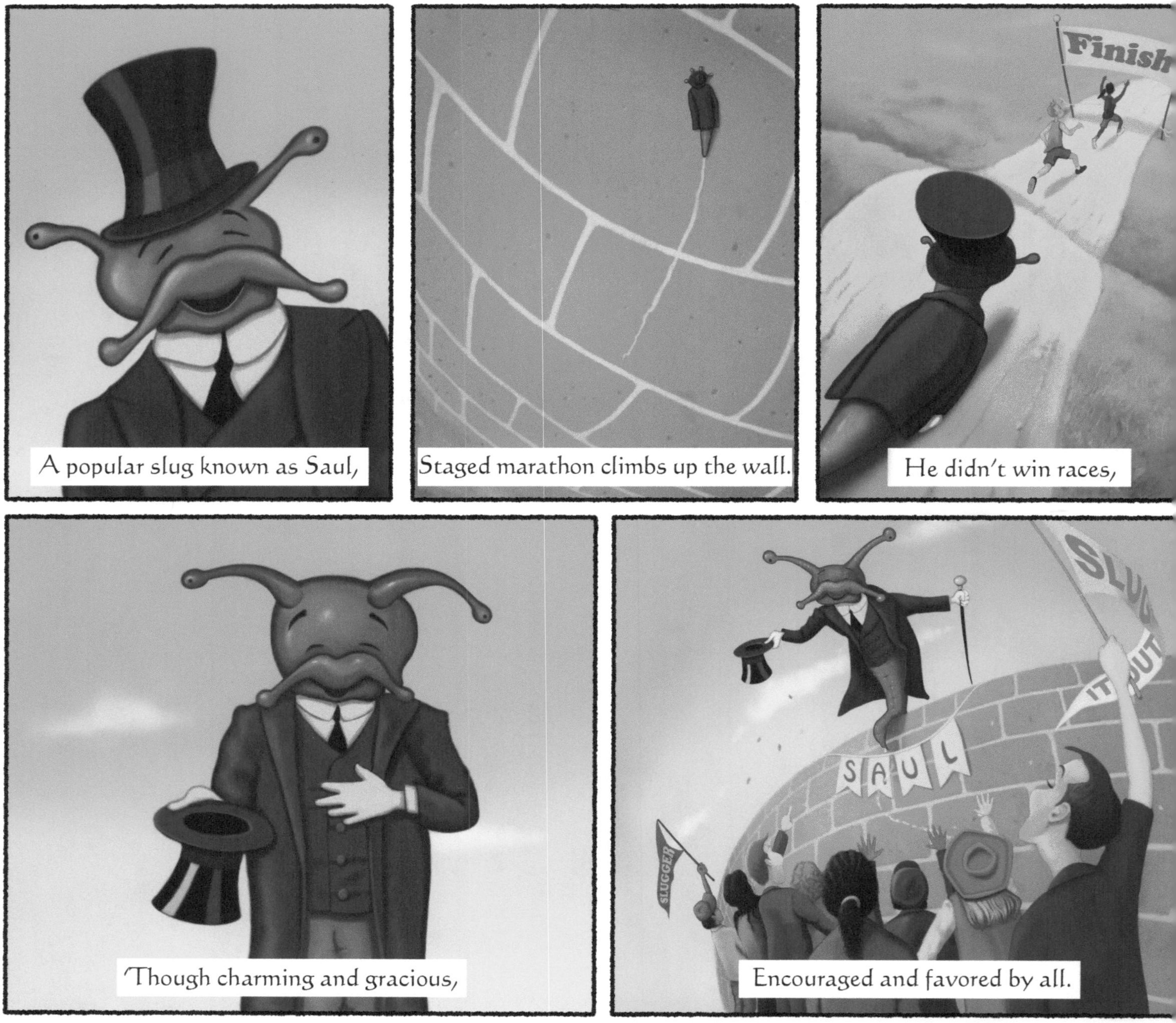
A popular slug known as Saul,
Staged marathon climbs up the wall.
Finish
He didn't win races,
'Though charming and gracious,
SAUL
SLUGGER
Encouraged and favored by all.

A slug is essentially a snail without a shell, and indeed a slow creature. Their average speed is only about two feet in 45 seconds. Most of the slug's body is a large muscle that serves as a foot. On the underside of its body, a series of muscles contract enabling it to creep. The slug's slime contains fibers which prevent it from sliding down vertical surfaces. This slimy secretion absorbs water, making it difficult to wash off your hands. Chemicals in the slime serve as a navigation system leading slugs home to their tunnel. The glistening, silver trail often seen is just dried slime. Slugs have green blood and possess one lung instead of two. A small hole on the right side of the body leads to the single lung. Slugs have two pairs of retractable tentacles on their head. The upper tentacles are equipped with light-sensitive eyespots on the ends that provide both vision and smell. Each eyestalk is capable of moving independently and can be re-grown if lost. The lower pair of tentacles is use for tasting and feeling.

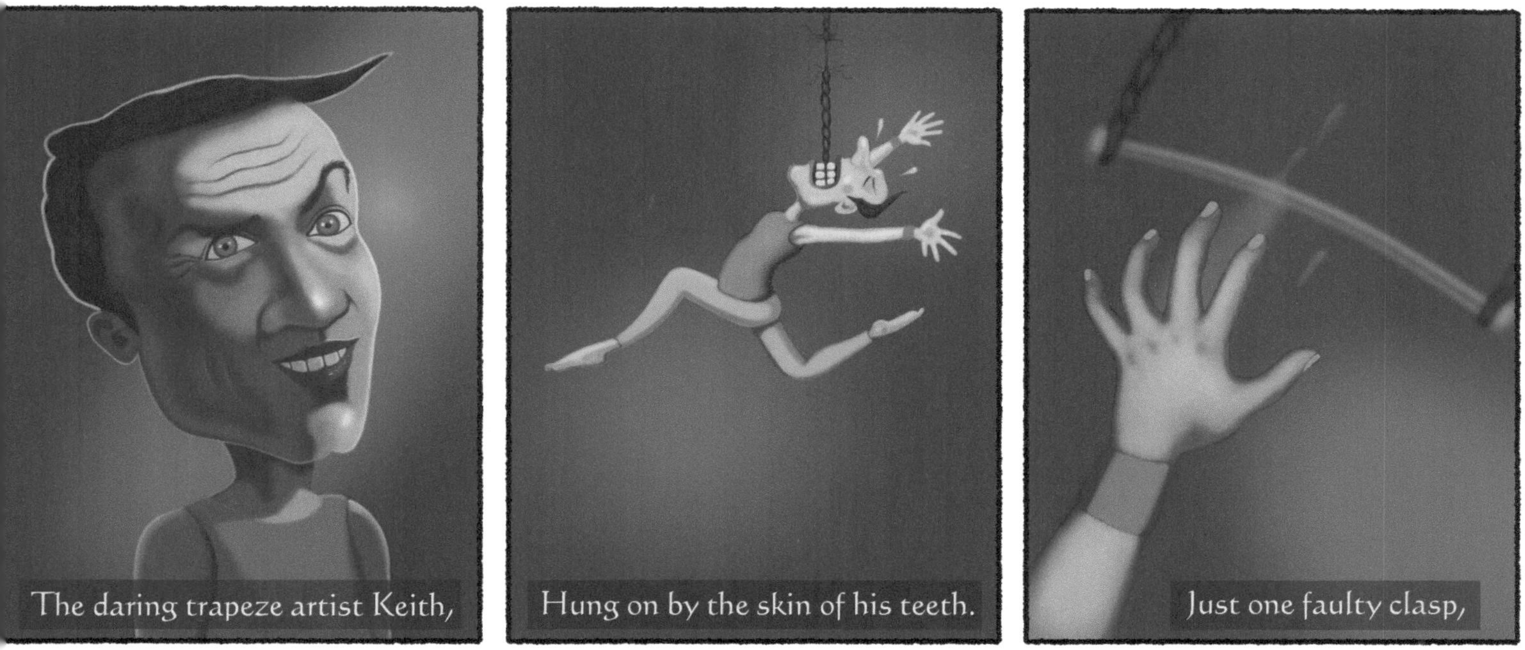
The daring trapeze artist Keith,
Hung on by the skin of his teeth.
Just one faulty clasp,

Caused patrons to gasp,

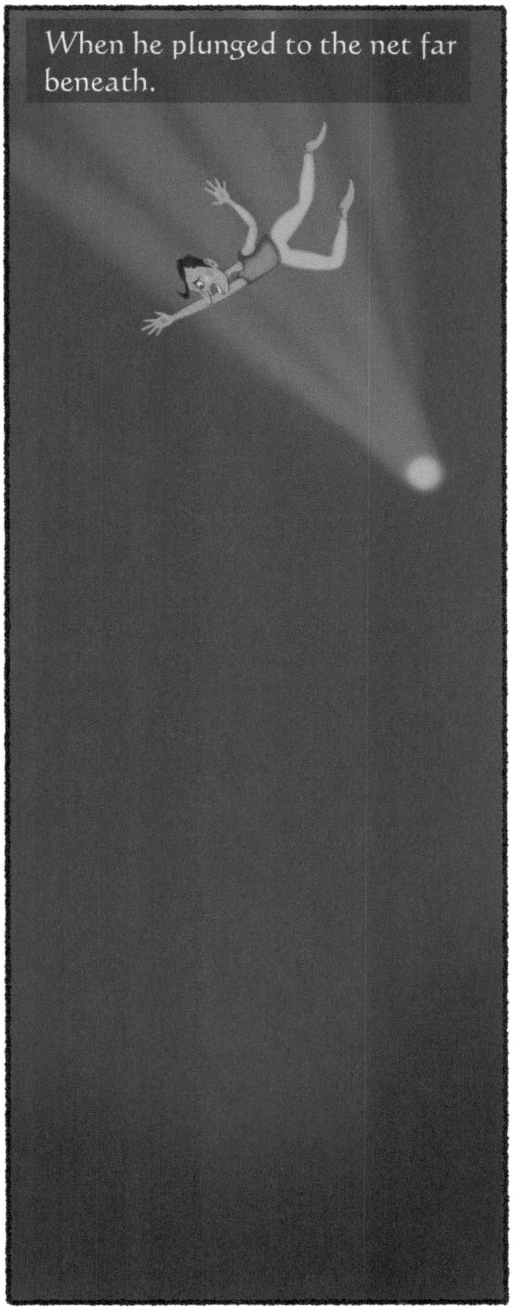
When he plunged to the net far beneath.

The French acrobat Jules Leotard performed the first flying trapeze act for Cirque Napoleon in Paris in 1859. He is credited with inventing the event after perfecting his routine soaring over a swimming pool. He bravely performed before audiences without a safety net, above mattresses spread on a raised platform below. Jules Leotard was the inspiration for the famous song, "The Daring Young Man on the Flying Trapeze." The skin-tight outfit he wore in his 1859 Paris debut became forever known as the "Leotard." Sadly, Jules Leotard lost his life around the age of 30 when he contracted an infectious disease thought to be smallpox. Shortly after his death, the first safety nets were introduced. The use of safety nets enabled audacious performers to attempt more dynamic routines involving greater risk, like multiple somersaults.

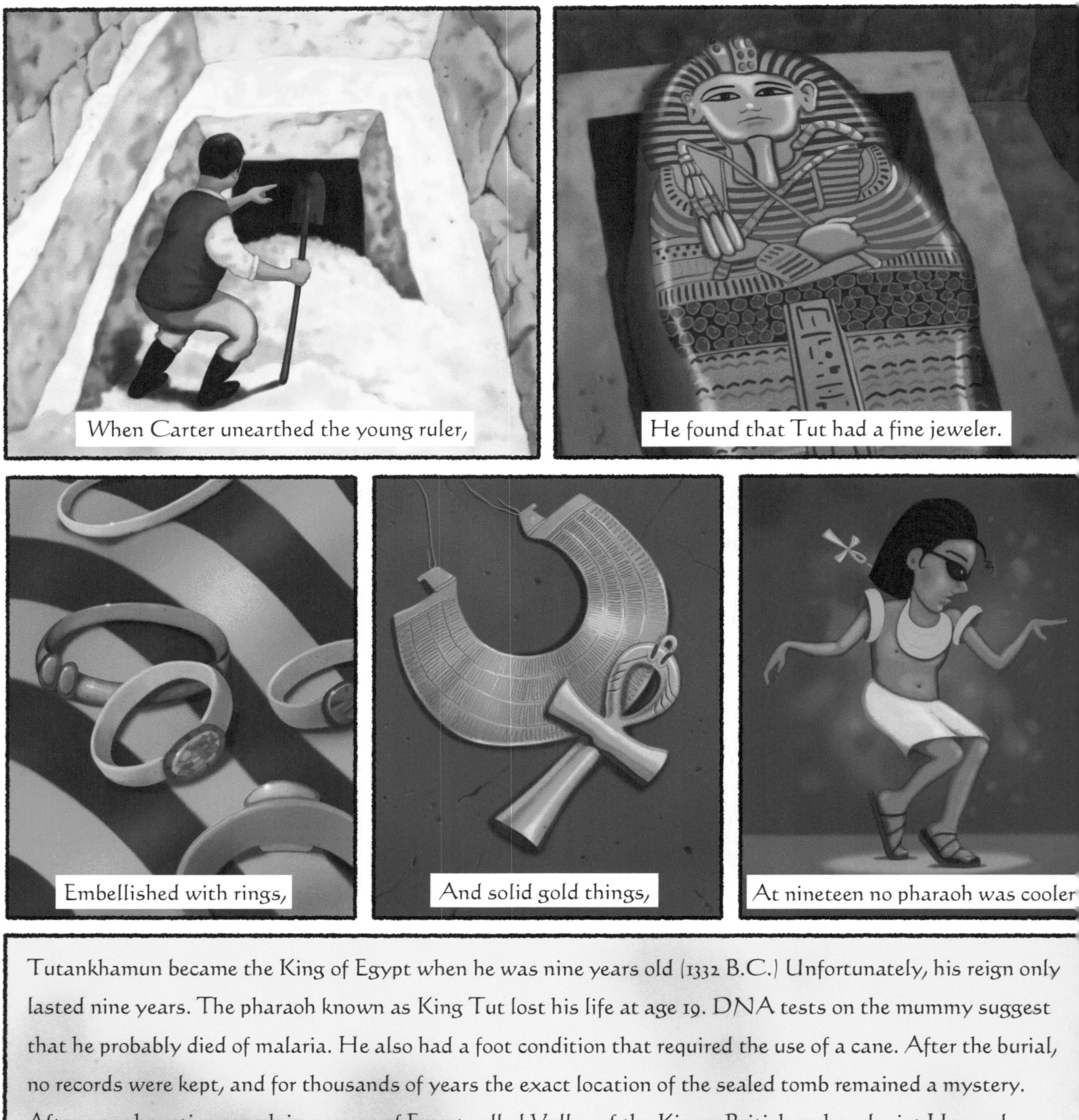
When Carter unearthed the young ruler,
He found that Tut had a fine jeweler.
Embellished with rings,
And solid gold things,
At nineteen no pharaoh was cooler

Tutankhamun became the King of Egypt when he was nine years old (1332 B.C.) Unfortunately, his reign only lasted nine years. The pharaoh known as King Tut lost his life at age 19. DNA tests on the mummy suggest that he probably died of malaria. He also had a foot condition that required the use of a cane. After the burial, no records were kept, and for thousands of years the exact location of the sealed tomb remained a mystery. After an exhaustive search in an area of Egypt called Valley of the Kings, British archaeologist Howard Carter discovered the inner chamber of the tomb in 1922. He was astonished to find the room intact and undisturbed after 3,000 years! Colorful murals graced the walls depicting Tut's funeral. A treasure trove of priceless artifacts was also found, including statues made of gold and ivory, precious jewelry, toys, perfumes, and oils. The stone sarcophagus holding the mummified remains of King Tut contained three coffins, one inside the other. The boy King was revealed in the innermost coffin made of solid gold! Buried with him was an array of lavish jewelry including bracelets, rings, and plenty of "bling."

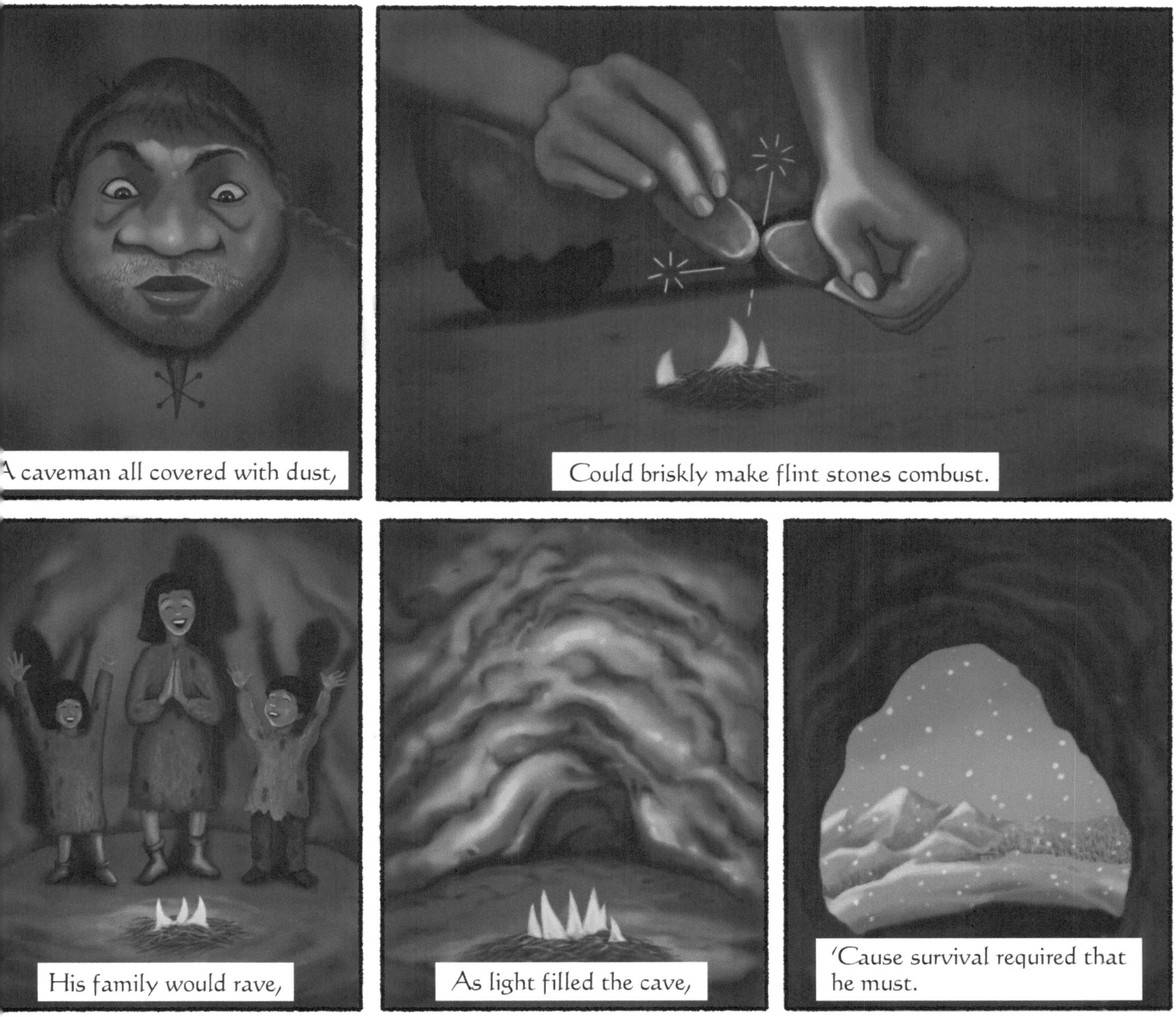
A caveman all covered with dust,
Could briskly make flint stones combust.
His family would rave,
As light filled the cave,
'Cause survival required that he must.

Learning to control and use fire was essential for the people of the Stone Age. A fire aided their survival and improved the quality of their lives in a multitude of ways. Besides providing warmth and comfort, fire enabled cave dwellers to enjoy cooked food that was easier to chew and digest than raw food, especially if they'd never visited a dentist. Cooking meat provided health benefits by killing harmful bacteria. Smoked meat could be preserved for later use. Clay fired ceramic pots were used to carry and store water and food. Our early ancestors discovered that animals were fearful of fire and used it to their advantage. They employed fire as a clever hunting tactic. Rather than confronting a massive beast with a primitive weapon, cavemen used fire to frighten animals causing them to stampede over a cliff, providing meat in abundance. Finally, the precious embers of a fire pit, safe from the threat of approaching animals, encouraged groups to gather together for social interaction. However, no artifacts have been found suggesting that the people of the Stone Age enjoyed s'mores.

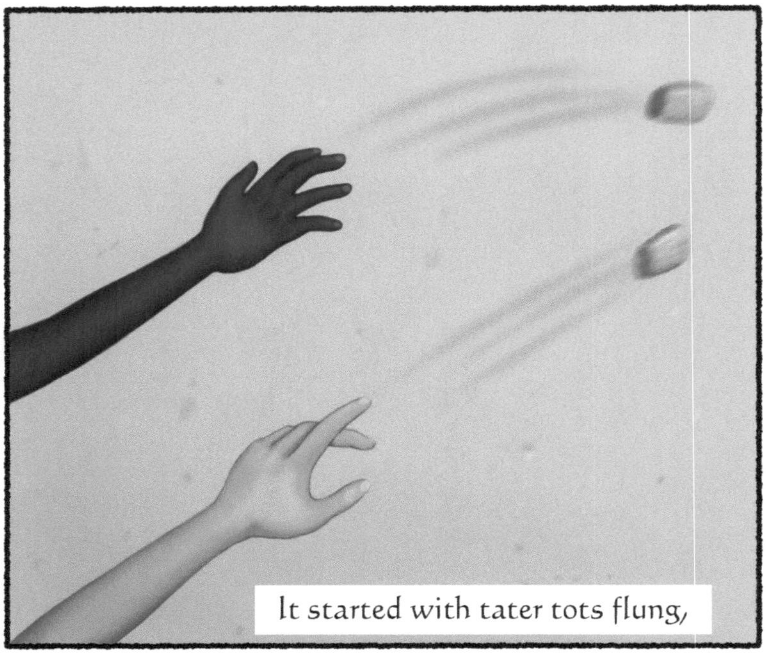
It started with tater tots flung,

At lunch today striking Butch Young.

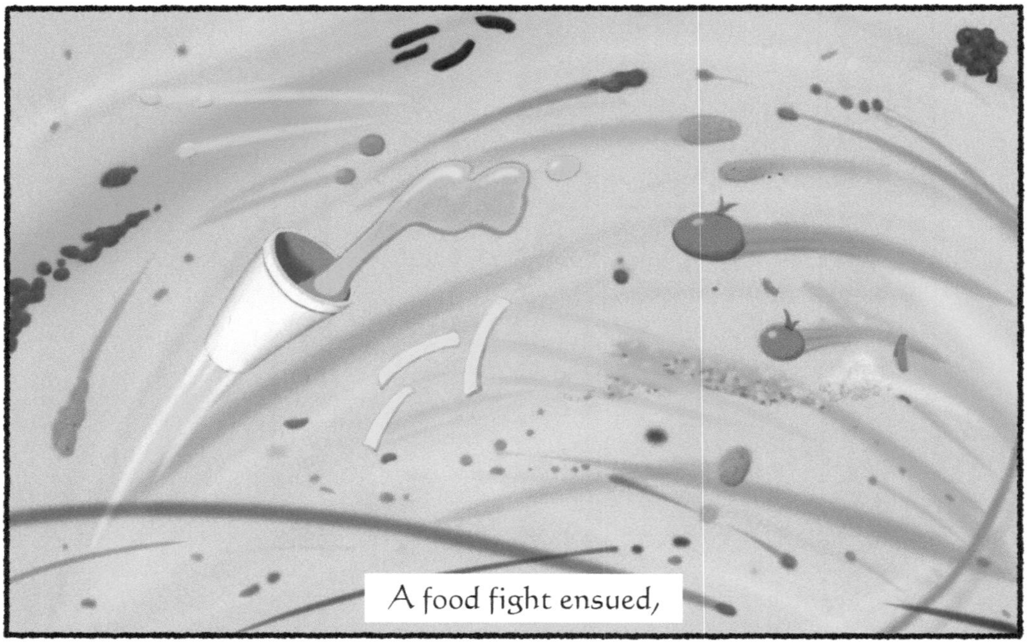
A food fight ensued,

With kids wearing food,

'Till loudly the final bell'd rung.

Throwing food in the school lunchroom is inappropriate. However, ther is one place where an annual festival is held, and thousands of people d just that. It happens in the small Spanish town of Bunol each August. Truckloads of tomatoes are brought to the center of town, and what is often referred to as "The World's Largest Food Fight" takes place. For one hour, participants splatter one another with a cross-fire of overripe tomatoes. After the melee, fire trucks are employed to spray down the streets. The good news is that after the tomato pulp is washed away, the acidity of tomatoes helps to clean the streets. So the next time vegetable matter whizzes past your ear in the school cafeteria resist the urge to retaliate. Instead, start saving money for a trip to Spain.

Unsinkable
They claimed that the ship wouldn't sink,

But not the great vessel you think.

This boat was gigantic,

TITAN
But not the Titanic,

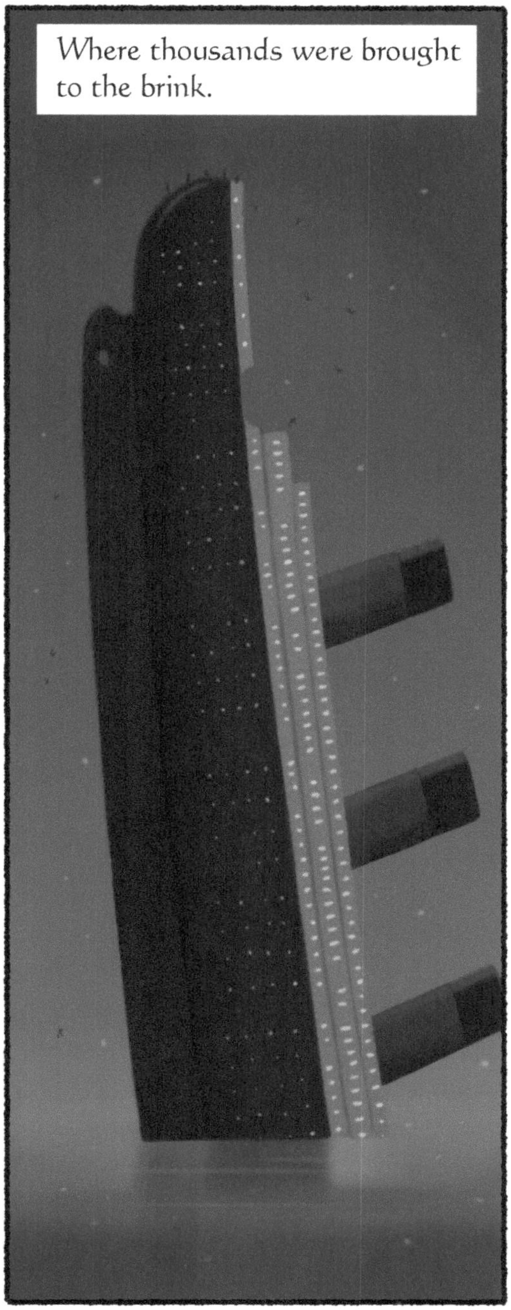
Where thousands were brought to the brink.

The story of that fateful maiden voyage of the British passenger liner Titanic is well known. But believe it or not, a full 14 years before the Titanic was declared the worst maritime disaster in modern history, American author Morgan Robertson published a novel titled, The Wreck of the Titan or, Futility. If you think the ship's name the Titan is an eerie coincidence, you may be astounded to learn just how many similarities were found in the novel, and the actual sinking of the Titanic more than a decade later. Both British-owned vessels were considered unsinkable with exactly 19 watertight compartments, and therefore carried less than half the number of lifeboats needed. Each ocean liner was made of steel, and struck an iceberg on the starboard side, in the North Atlantic Ocean. Both events occurred near the stroke of midnight on an evening in April, approximately 400 miles south of Newfoundland!

There once was an ambitious ant,
Quite weary of hearing,
"You can't."
To prove that he could,
So proudly he stood,
With leaves of a piggyback plant.

Ants and humans share a reputation for exhibiting strength and hard work. You could say ants outperform Olympic weightlifters as ants can lift more than fifty times their own weight. In fact, Asian weaver ants can carry loads one hundred times their own body weight! Relative to their size, the muscles of ants are thicker than those of larger animals. Additionally, ants share an unusual trait with mankind. Humans and ants are among the few inhabitants of earth that farm other creatures. Similar to the way we raise cows for milk, ants also do this with other insects, mainly aphids. Aphids suck the sap of plants and secrete a substance called honeydew. Ants love to feed upon the tasty honeydew so they become farmers by protecting the aphids from their natural predators. During periods of heavy rain, ants provide shelter to the aphids or their eggs in their nests. These practices ensure a plentiful supply of honeydew. We know that ants once lived alongside the dinosaurs because scientists found fossilized ants encased in amber. The golden colored substance was formed when resin from trees became hardened and remained preserved for nearly 100 million years!

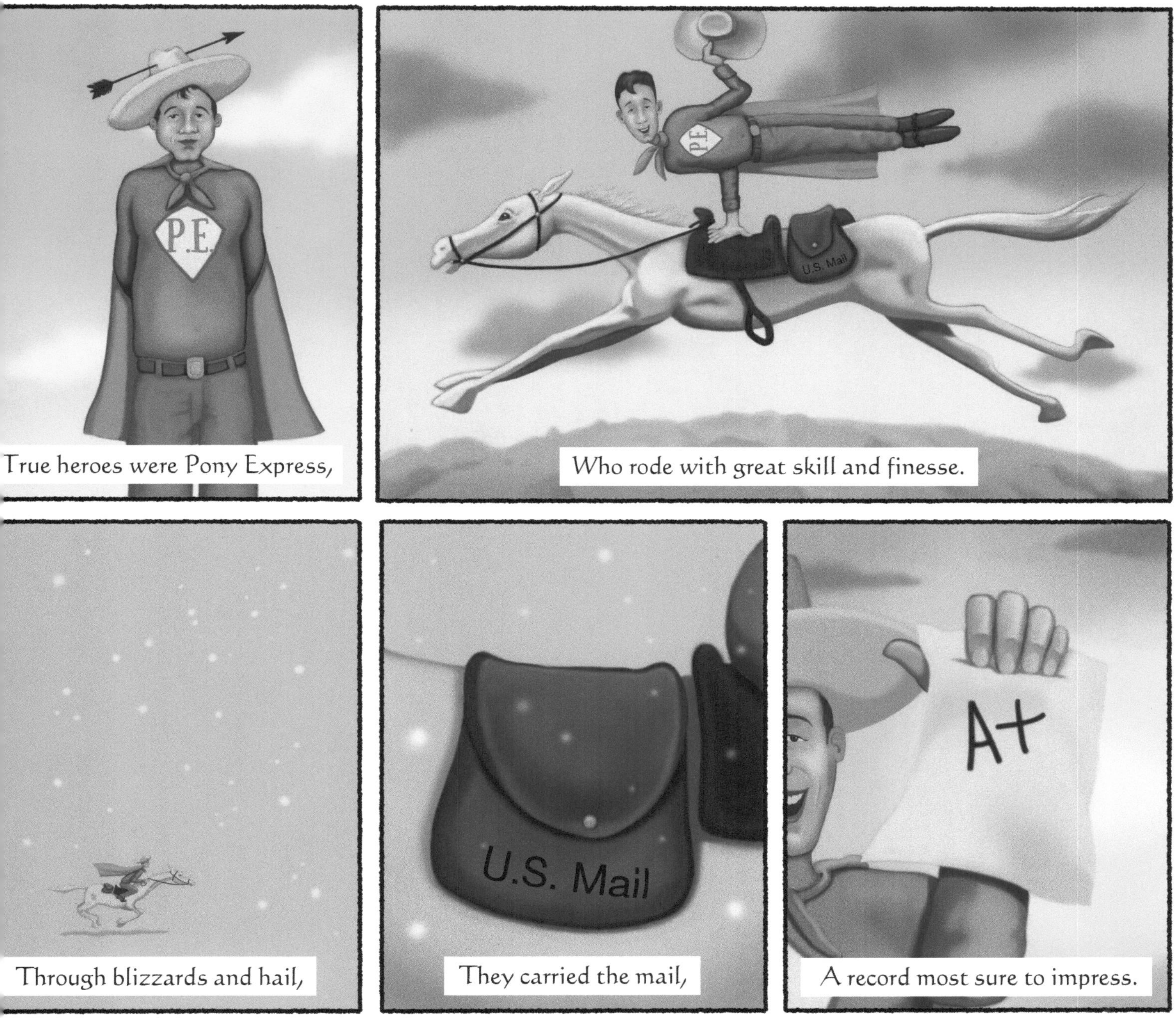

True heroes were Pony Express,
P.E.
Who rode with great skill and finesse.
P.E.
U.S. Mail
Through blizzards and hail,
U.S. Mail
They carried the mail,
A+
A record most sure to impress.

the mid 19th century, more than a hundred years before the arrival of e-mail, it took twenty-five days to send ail across the country to California by stagecoach. Steamships also transported mail, but the trip around outh America took even longer. The Pony Express was an overland mail service from St. Joseph, Missouri to an Francisco. This continuous horse and rider relay required only ten days. The journey covered more than 000 miles, and was linked by 190 transfer stations operated by an attendant with a fresh supply of horses. ach valiant rider changed horses every 10-15 miles tossing a special mailbag called a mochila onto a new mount r a speedy transfer. Individual riders traveled 75 - 100 miles a day. These daring men and teenagers faced harsh eather and unforgiving terrain, along with the threat of attacks by thieves. The Pony Express was only in ervice for 18 months. In that time they delivered over 34,000 parcels and only one mochila was lost! This record reliable service was truly astonishing. The Pony Express ceased operations in 1861 when Western Union began uccessful transcontinental telegraph service.

Lamplighters helped the fine people each night,
Walk dark streets of London without any fright.
With each lamp left glowing,
They took pride in knowing,
The city was safely alight.

In London, in the days before public lighting was available, the streets at night were dark and dangerous. Brave citizens who ventured out after dark often hired the services of "link-boys." These lads walked in front of their guests holding a stick with a burning rag fueled by tar. Link-boys were often poor street urchins and orphans looking to earn a few farthings, a sum of one-fourth of a British penny. The first public city lights were fueled by oil derived from fish and whales. These lamps left a foul odor and were inadequate to light a city the size of London, whose population had swelled to over a million by 1800. Fortunately, they were soon replaced by gas lamps. The lamplighters of the Victorian era provided a valuable service turning night into day. Into the approaching dusk each evening, the lamplighter carried a ladder and an 8-foot brass pole with a pilot light. They made their rounds lighting scores of lamps, only to return every morning at dawn to extinguish them.

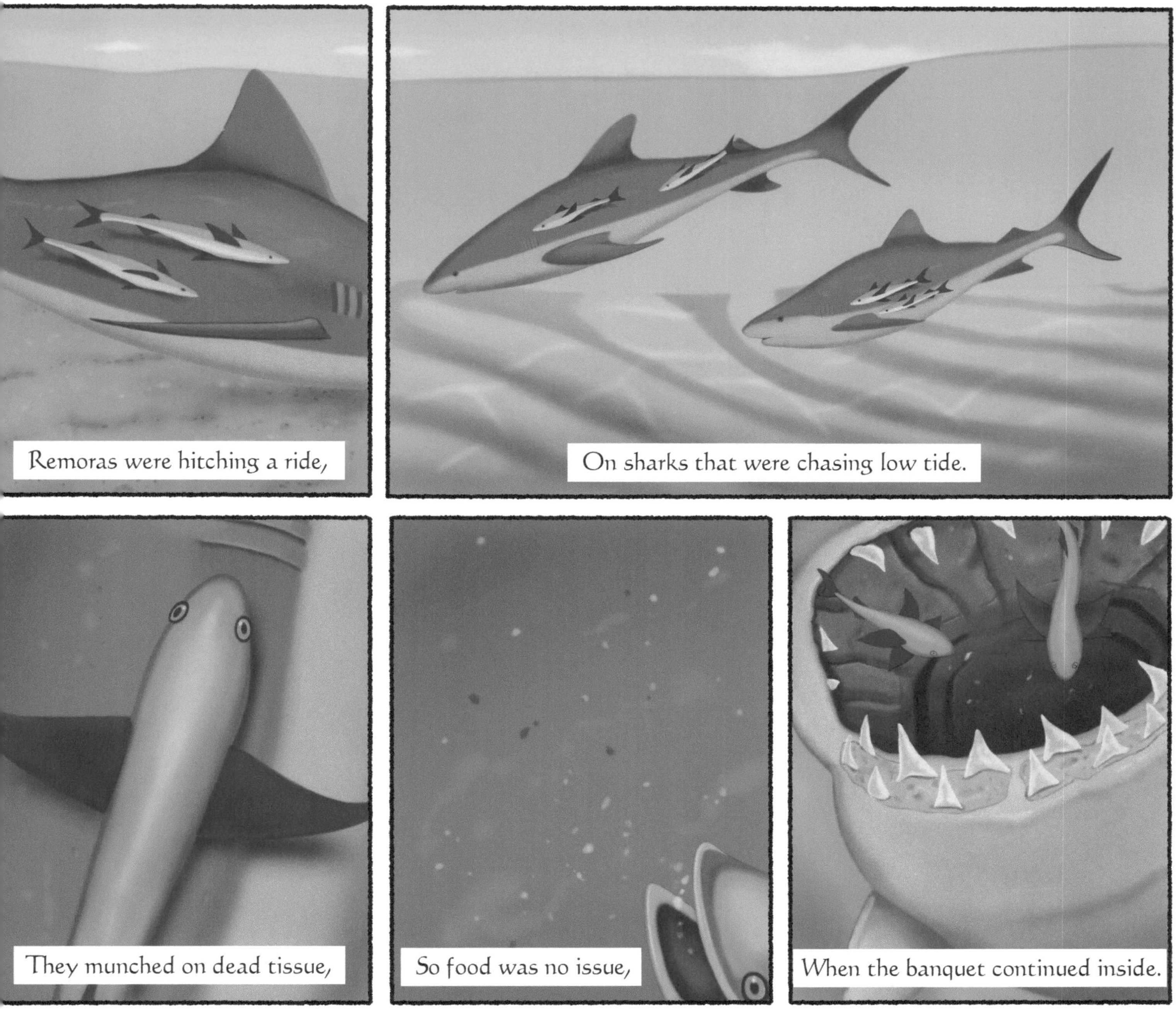
Remoras were hitching a ride,
On sharks that were chasing low tide.
They munched on dead tissue,
So food was no issue,
When the banquet continued inside.

The remora, often called a suckerfish, is a curious marine creature. Remoras inhabit tropical waters and like to attach themselves and "hitchhike" a ride on sharks, whales, sea turtles, rays, and a variety of other larger fish. They accomplish this by employing a mighty sucker-like organ that resembles the tread of an athletic shoe. Remoras eat leftovers and remove parasites, bacteria, and dead skin tissue from their host. Smaller remoras actually live inside the mouths of whales, larger sharks, and manta rays where they feed on bacteria and food scraps. Besides sea creatures, remoras have been known to latch onto the bottom of boats, and even to scuba divers! Remoras benefit from riding along with their host because the movement provides a constant flow of water across their gills aiding respiration. Many cultures around the world have used the remora to harvest sea turtles and fish. Fishermen tie a fishing line to a remora. Once released into the water, the remora attaches itself to a host. The fisherman then pulls both creatures from the water.

While riding the coaster at Fun World,
We sped with a whoosh and a whirl
We swooped from the crest,
And I must confess.
I seriously started to hurl.

The modern roller coaster originated in Russia when sled riders descended the winter slopes in wood-framed ice slides. They adapted this activity to summertime by sending wheeled carts down wooden ramps. The evolution continued in France where wheels were added to the sleds and attached to a track. In 1872, in the mountains of Pennsylvania, a track built to transport coal was discontinued and transformed into a scenic tour. After a second track was added, the railway became known as the Mauch Chunk, Summit Hill, and Switchback Railway. The attraction offered breathtaking views of the Lehigh River. At the time it was one of the most popular tourist attractions in the United States. Then in 1884 at Coney Island, New York, daring riders could pay a nickel to climb to the pinnacle of a tower, and ride a car that dropped 600 feet. On a rippled track, the car reached a top speed of just 6 miles per hour. The 1920s ushered in the Golden Age of roller coasters when more than 1,500 wooden coasters were constructed in parks across America. These coasters reached speeds of 40-60 miles per hour. Many featured a series of drops called a camelback. At these speeds, the sudden dips provided that stomach-in-your-throat sensation that thrill seekers crave.

The bat in the belfry named Joe,
Quite often knew not where to go.
Although he was blind,
He listened to find,
The pulsating echo below.

A belfry, or church bell tower, is often infested with bats because it offers darkness and seclusion. Bats are the only mammals with the capability of continuous flight. There are two types of bats. Microbats really are "as blind as a bat," and use echolocation to navigate during their search for food. Microbats emit noises to determine the relative distance of nearby objects by how quickly the sound waves bounce back to them. This type of active sonar is used by submarines. In contrast, fruit bats, or flying foxes, are equipped with large eyes designed for vision. Bats provide a nontoxic pest control service by eating several thousand insects each night. The hungry bats help farmers by controlling the population of harmful insects that destroy crops. Vampire bats have small, extremely sharp teeth, capable of piercing an animal's skin without them noticing. They mainly target cattle and deer.

That daring old steeplejack Howard,
Was never considered a coward.
He'd perch on a steeple,
And wave to the people,
As over the city he towered.

Steeplejacks and ironworkers know what it's like to be Spiderman. Steeplejacks inspect, maintain, and repair al types of vertical structures like church spires, industrial chimneys, bell and clock towers, buildings, and bridges; whereas, ironworkers are mainly involved in construction. In 1886, a railroad bridge was being constructed over the St. Lawrence River onto a portion of Mohawk reservation land. An agreement was reached permitting use of the land in exchange for jobs for the tribesmen as laborers during construction. After work, these curious men were known to venture upon the towering steel beams and girders, showing no fear of the dangerous heights. Soon many were trained for better-paying jobs as riveters. Then in the early part of the 20th century, many Mohawk Indians from reservations in and around Canada migrated to New York City to erect the city's skyscrapers and bridges. These intrepid, native North Americans made valuable contributions to every major high steel construction project in the city including the Empire State Building, the Chrysler Building, Rockefell Center, and the George Washington Bridge.

At Stanford, a fruit fly named Devin,

Soon died and ascended to Heaven.

ARRIVALS
RAY FARGO 10:35 ARRIVED
ROSE TOPEKA 10:45 ON TIME
DEVIN STANFORD 11:00 LATE
LOUIS ALBANY 11:10 ON TIME
EVA MIAMI 11:30 ON TIME
OTIS RALEIGH 11:40 ON TIME
And when he arrived,

Pete told him aside,

"We expected you here by eleven."

We owe a great debt of gratitude to fruit flies. They have long served as model organisms in biological research facilities around the world because 75% of the genes that cause diseases in humans are also found in fruit flies. For example, in one clinical study researchers found that fruit flies that were given too much sugar developed the identical symptoms of Type 2 diabetes as humans. Fruit flies only live about 45 days on average. Their lifespan is so short that scientists can easily study successive generations in just a few months. Fruit flies played a vital role in medical research studying diabetes, cancer, Alzheimer's, and Parkinson's disease. So the next time you're in the kitchen feeling annoyed by a swarm of fruit flies hovering above the overripe peaches, perhaps a simple thank you is in order.

The honorable mayor of L.A.

Once spoke in a flimsy toupee.

While wicked winds blew,

His aides applied glue,

But never could get it to stay.

The mayor is the highest ranking officer in the municipal government of a city or town. The office of mayor is an elected position. The mayor works closely with the city council. They are responsible for local services such as the water supply, sewer, garbage disposal, sidewalks, roads, building codes, zoning, parks, playgrounds, and libraries. Toupees and wigs have long been used in many cultures throughout the world as a solution for thinning hair and baldness. The ancient Egyptians wore them for other reasons as when toupees were adorned as a sign of wealth, and also worn for protection from the blazing, desert sun.

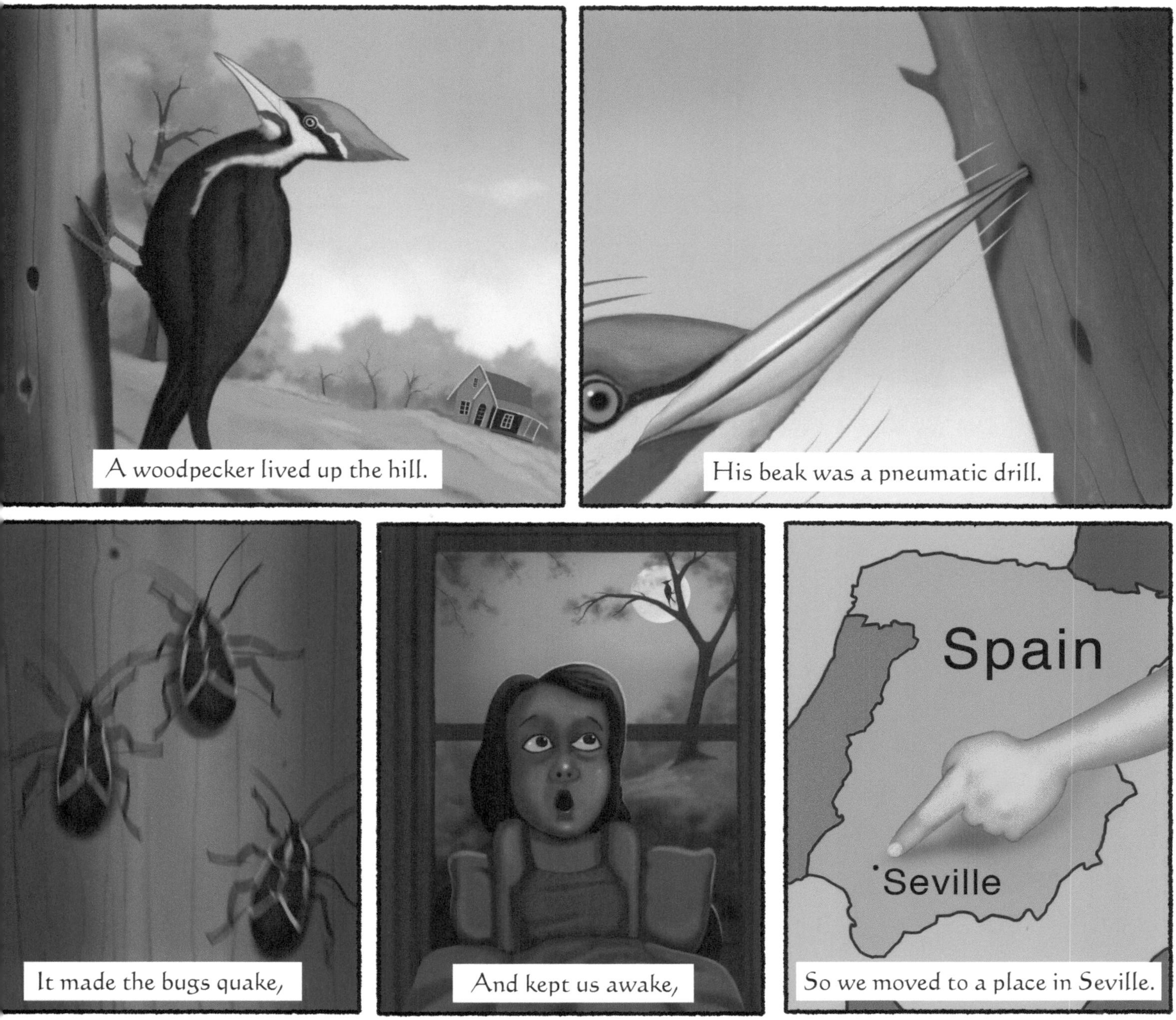
A woodpecker lived up the hill.
His beak was a pneumatic drill.
It made the bugs quake,
And kept us awake,
Spain
Seville
So we moved to a place in Seville.

irds are gifted construction workers. Many species skillfully gather twigs, grass, moss, and leaves to build nest. Most of the 180 species of woodpeckers live in wooded forest habitats, and use their powerful bills to xcavate a cavity into a tree for nesting. Their beak serves as a chisel to penetrate tree bark to expose tasty isects and release the flow of sap. Woodpeckers have an unusually long tongue--nearly four inches in ength--equipped with a sticky substance on the tip that helps them to catch insects. The tongue length is among everal unique special adaptations that protect the woodpecker from brain damage while pecking twenty times er second, for a total of about 10,000 times a day. The entire tongue is wrapped around the inside of the skull to often the impact of pounding. Together with sponge-like skull bones, powerful neck muscles, a flexible spine, nd unequal lengths of the upper and lower bill, this persistent worker needs no hard hat. Occasionally in the pring, woodpeckers pound resonant surfaces to mark territory or to attract a mate. This hammering often occurs n house siding and gutters. The raucous ruckus can reverberate through your house, and if you're not one who ses early with the birds, you soon will be!

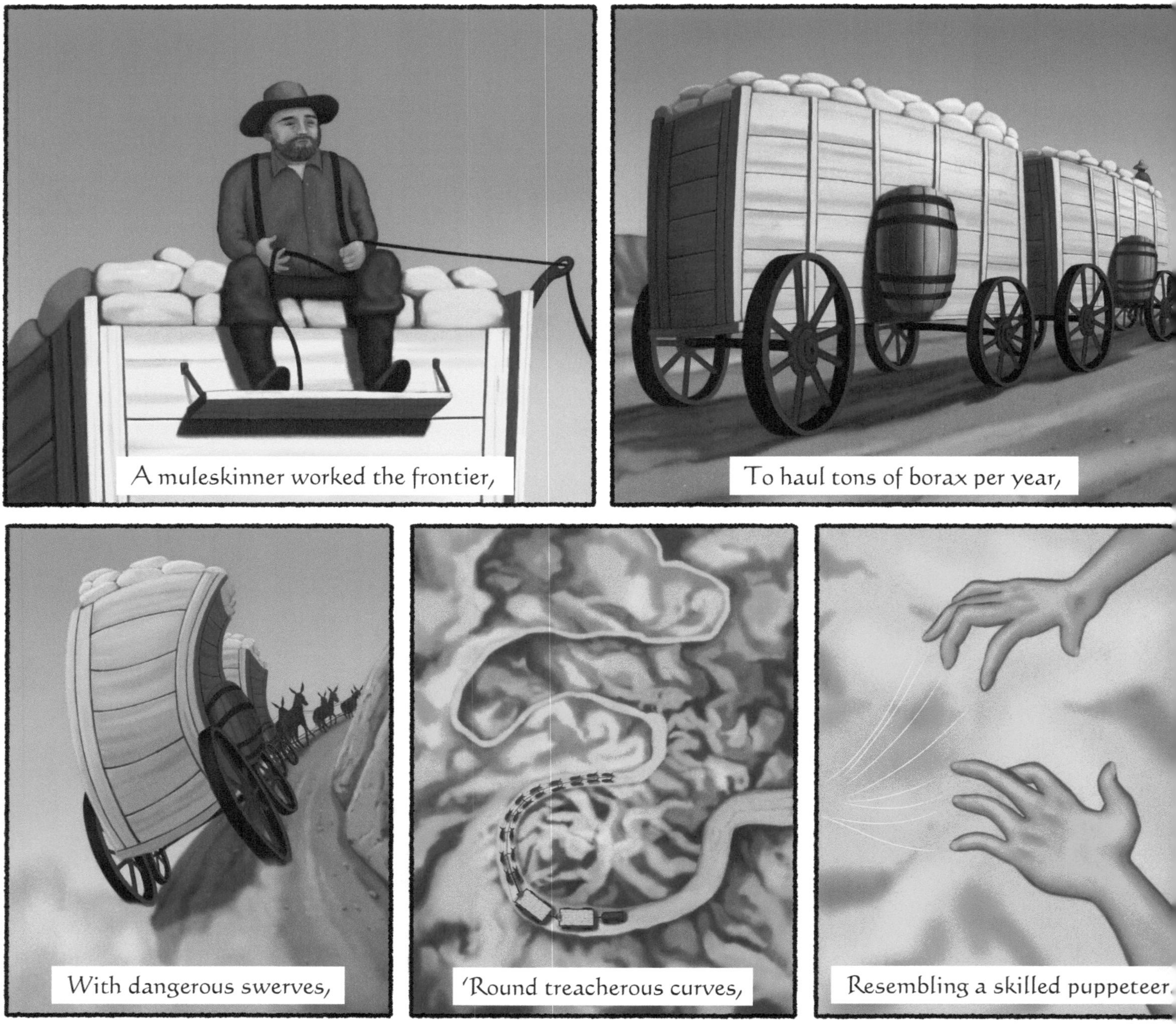
A muleskinner worked the frontier,
To haul tons of borax per year,
With dangerous swerves,
'Round treacherous curves,
Resembling a skilled puppeteer.

Twenty-mule teams were actually teams of eighteen mules and two horses attached to large wagons. From 1883-1889 they endured the scorching desert heat while hauling more than 20 million pounds of borax ore from the mines in Death Valley to the railroad in Mojave, California, 165 miles away. Borax is a mineral used to make laundry soap because it effectively eliminates stains, and controls odors naturally. The driver of a team of mules was known as a "muleskinner." Like an expert puppeteer, he masterfully controlled the team by using a single rope called a "jerk line," along with verbal commands, and a long whip called a "black snake." The stamina and ingenuity of man and mule were severely tested when required to traverse the dangerous curves of the Panamint Mountains. To keep the long center chain going around a sharp curve and to avoid pulling the team over the edge, some of the mules were trained to step over the chain and pull at an angle away from the curve, completing the turn. In the six years that they made the perilous, twenty-day round- trip journey, not a single animal or wagon was lost!

A hard working mason named Clay,
Once watched a dog ruin his day.
On damp, wet concrete,
KEEP OFF!
That mutt tapped his feet,
Performing a canine ballet.

Various forms of concrete have been used in construction for more than 2,000 years. The Roman Empire had roadways, aqueducts, and some buildings made with a primitive mixture of concrete. The substance was composed of gravel and coarse sand, blended with heated lime and water. Horsehair and animal blood were also added. Modern concrete is a mixture of rock, sand, gravel, water, and Portland cement. Portland cement was invented by a British stonemason named Joseph Aspdin in his own kitchen. The innovative inventor obtained a patent for his discovery in 1824. He applied heat to a finely ground, powdered mixture of limestone and clay. With the addition of water, it hardened into durable cement. Aspdin named the product Portland cement because it resembled a stone found on the Isle of Portland, in the English Channel. Portland cement has since revolutionized the construction industry with endless applications.

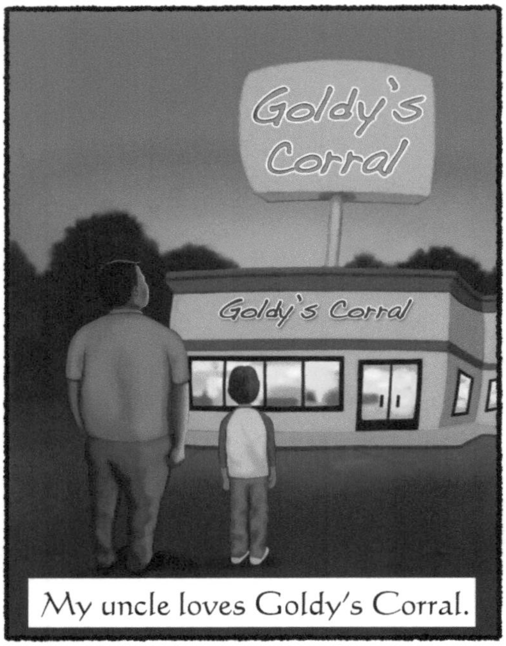

Goldy's Corral
Goldy's Corral
My uncle loves Goldy's Corral.

His plate a tall stratified pile.

The cascading fountains,

Make thick chocolate mountains,

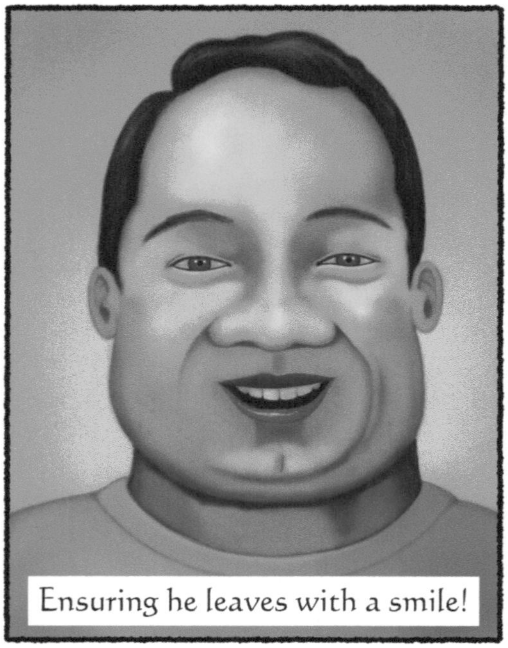
Ensuring he leaves with a smile!

A healthy diet involves making wise nutritional food choices along with balanced portions. Nutritional decisions can be easily influenced by persuasive advertising, convenient fast food outlets, and tempting buffet restaurants. When eating, it takes your brain about twenty minutes to signal that you are full, and when you take in more food than can be burned, it is stored as fat. Kids don't always grow at a steady rate. Occasional growth spurts occur with the rapid development of muscle and bone mass, especially around the start of the teenage years. That's why it's so important to get quality sleep each night, exercise daily, and drink plenty of water instead of sweetened drinks. Selecting foods from each of the basic food groups can provide the essential vitamins, energy, and fuel needed for optimum growth and development.

The notorious pirate named Sadie,

A swashbuckling buccaneer lady,

YE OLDE
LOST &
FOUND
Once lost her left ear,

While sipping a beer,

Then famously growled,
"Ahoy Matey!"

Unlike most pirates that roamed the open seas, Sadie "the Goat" Farrell and her rowdy band sailed up and down the Hudson River plundering small villages, farmhouses, and riverfront mansions. She was also known to kidnap people for ransom. Sadie earned her nickname "the Goat" from her favored practice of head-butting her foes. She met her match when she encountered a woman named Gallus Mag. Gallus, who stood over 6 feet tall, earned a living serving as a bouncer at a New York City tavern. She removed unruly patrons from the building by clutching their ear between her teeth. If they resisted, she bit off the auricle and added it to her collection stored in a jar of alcohol behind the bar. A fateful dispute with Mag resulted in the loss of Sadie's ear. Eventually, the two settled their differences, and the ear was later returned to Sadie preserved and pickled. Sadie then proudly displayed the ear in a locket worn around her neck for the rest of her life.

There once was a huge "thunder lizard,"
Possessing a muscular gizzard
Through forests, he'd wallow,
For stones which to swallow,
Digesting green plants like a wiza

The brontosaurus, now referred to as Apatosaurus, was a herbivore that devoured ample quantities of plants to maintain its enormous weight. Apatosaurus didn't chew its food. It swallowed chunks of plants, and ingested stones called gastroliths into its stomach to assist with digestion. The "thunder lizard" possessed a specialized stomach called a gizzard, made of thick walls of muscle used for grinding up food with the help of these stones. A number of modern animals including crocodiles, alligators, seals, and birds ingest stomach stones. This process is especially helpful to birds since they don't have teeth. Birds fill their stomachs with tin jagged rocks, grit, and shell fragments. These items serve as teeth as the gizzard muscle pulsates and contract Over time, when the stones become too smooth to grind effectively, they are regurgitated and replaced with a new supply. Ostriches have been known to swallow stones nearly four inches in length!

The smitten young octopus Lily,

Was love-struck and thought to be silly.

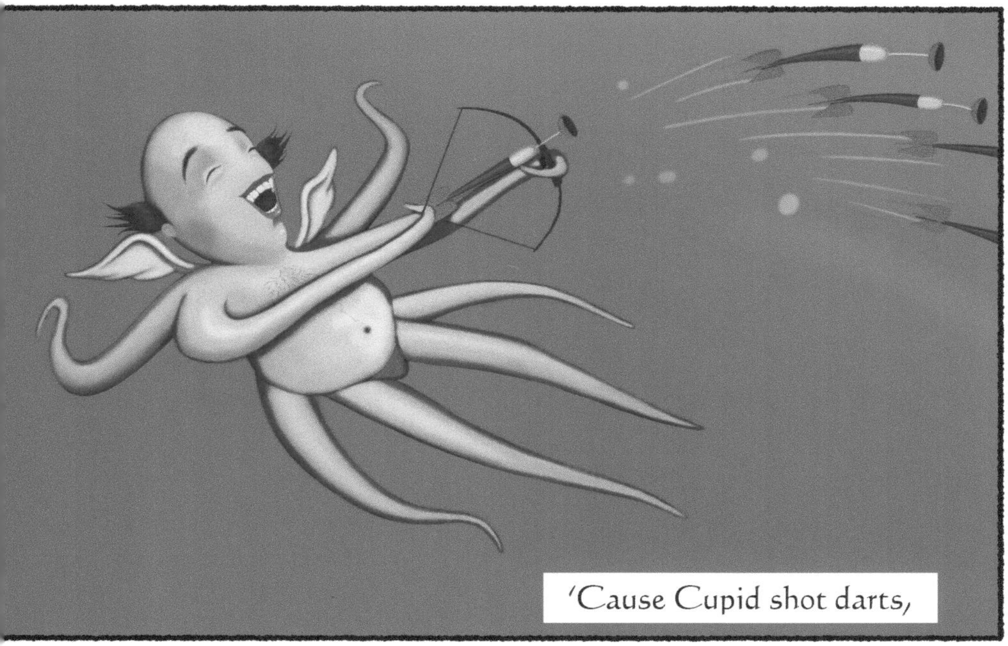
'Cause Cupid shot darts,

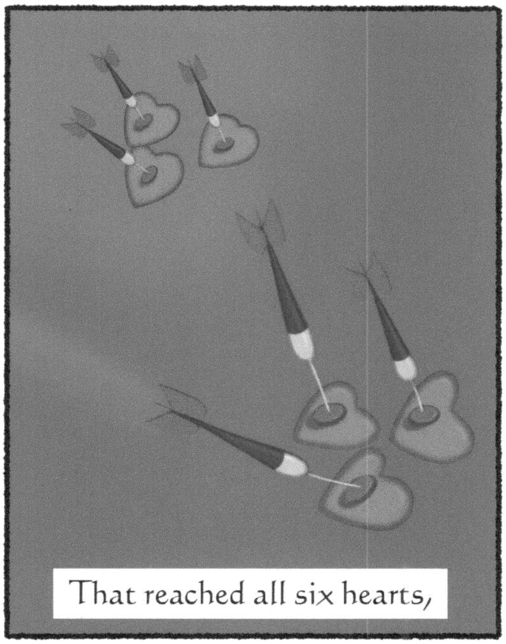
That reached all six hearts,

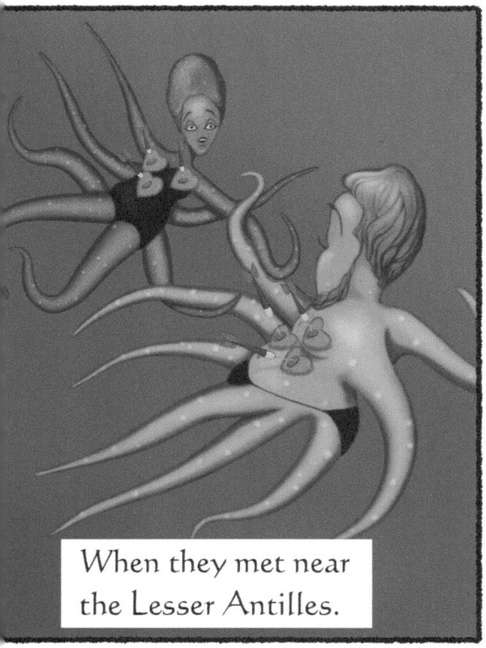
When they met near
the Lesser Antilles.

The Lesser Antilles is the name given to a group of islands in the Caribbean Sea. Octopuses have three operational hearts. Two hearts pump blood through each of the two gills, while a third circulates blood throughout the invertebrate's body. Octopuses actually have blue blood because the blood is copper-based. The dark ink they emit not only allows them to hide from predators, but it also contains a compound that causes a blinding irritation when sprayed into the eyes of an enemy. It also impairs a predator's sense of taste and smell, making it harder to track the fleeing octopus. The ink is so potent that the octopus must also escape the toxic cloud, or risk injury or death. Octopuses collect shells and other objects that are arranged around their solitary den in a type of garden.

The circus clowns came in their Jeeps,
With comical antics and leaps.
In petrified fear,
I watched the crowd cheer,
'Cause freakish clowns give me the creeps.

The role of the clown has always been to amuse the audience and make people laugh; nevertheless, many people feel uncomfortable in the presence of clowns. So if you find yourself among them, you're not alone. The fear of clowns is known as coulrophobia. There are three recognized types of clowns: *Whiteface*, *Auguste*, and Tramp. The *Whiteface* clown is the oldest, dating back to Greek theatre. They cover their face with white greasepaint and add color to emphasize the eyes and mouth. The Auguste clown is the zaniest clown, known for exaggerations in appearance. For example, they often wear oversized shoes and neckties. Their mouth and eyes are enlarged, punctuated by a round, scarlet red nose. In the traditional role, the Auguste clown serves as *Whiteface's* helper, and often endures the brunt of his pranks. Tramp clowns, as you might expect, are the sad clowns. Their hobo costumes are traditionally tattered and torn, and the face makeup worn is similar to the Auguste clown.

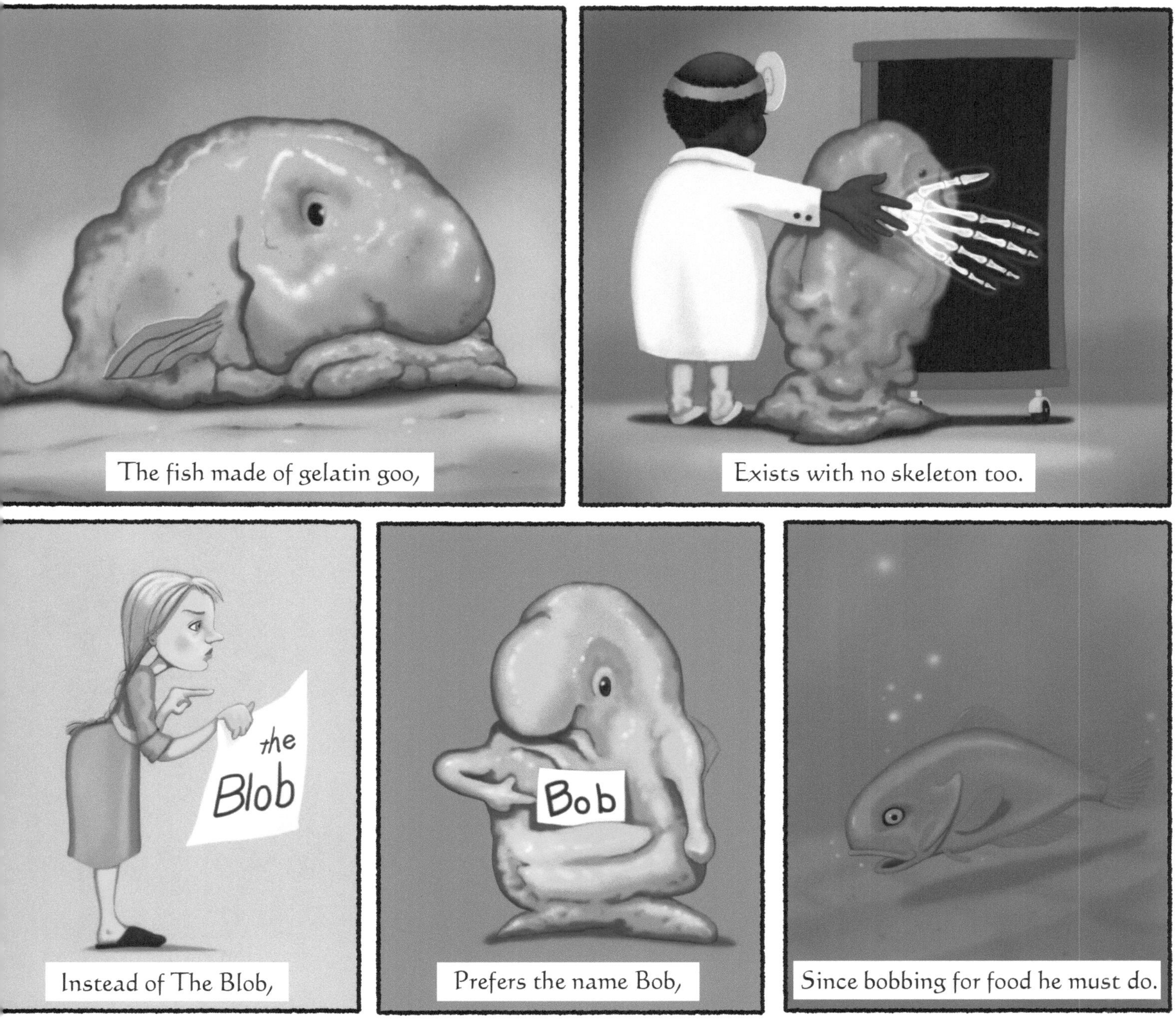
The fish made of gelatin goo,
Exists with no skeleton too.
the Blob
Instead of The Blob,
Bob
Prefers the name Bob,
Since bobbing for food he must do.

lobfish are deep sea dwellers found in the waters off New Zealand, Australia, and Tasmania. Their appearance, hen removed from the water is unattractive. They look like a giant tadpole made from a mass of pink gelatin, ith puffy, loose skin. Blobfish have small, beady eyes, and wear a permanent scowl. Over their plump lips hangs flap that resembles a human nose. Since blobfish lack muscle mass and a skeleton, they appear droopy when moved from the water. However, when subjected to extreme pressure at ocean depths of 3,000 feet, blobfish look ke ordinary fish. Blobfish cannot actively swim and must conserve energy, so they merely bob along the ocean oor sucking up small crustaceans floating nearby. Unfortunately, blobfish are endangered because they often ecome entrapped in fishing nets used to harvest more commercially desirable seafood like lobsters and crabs. The lob was the title of a classic science fiction movie featuring a menacing, gelatinous, alien life form that invaded small town, and consumed everything in its path.

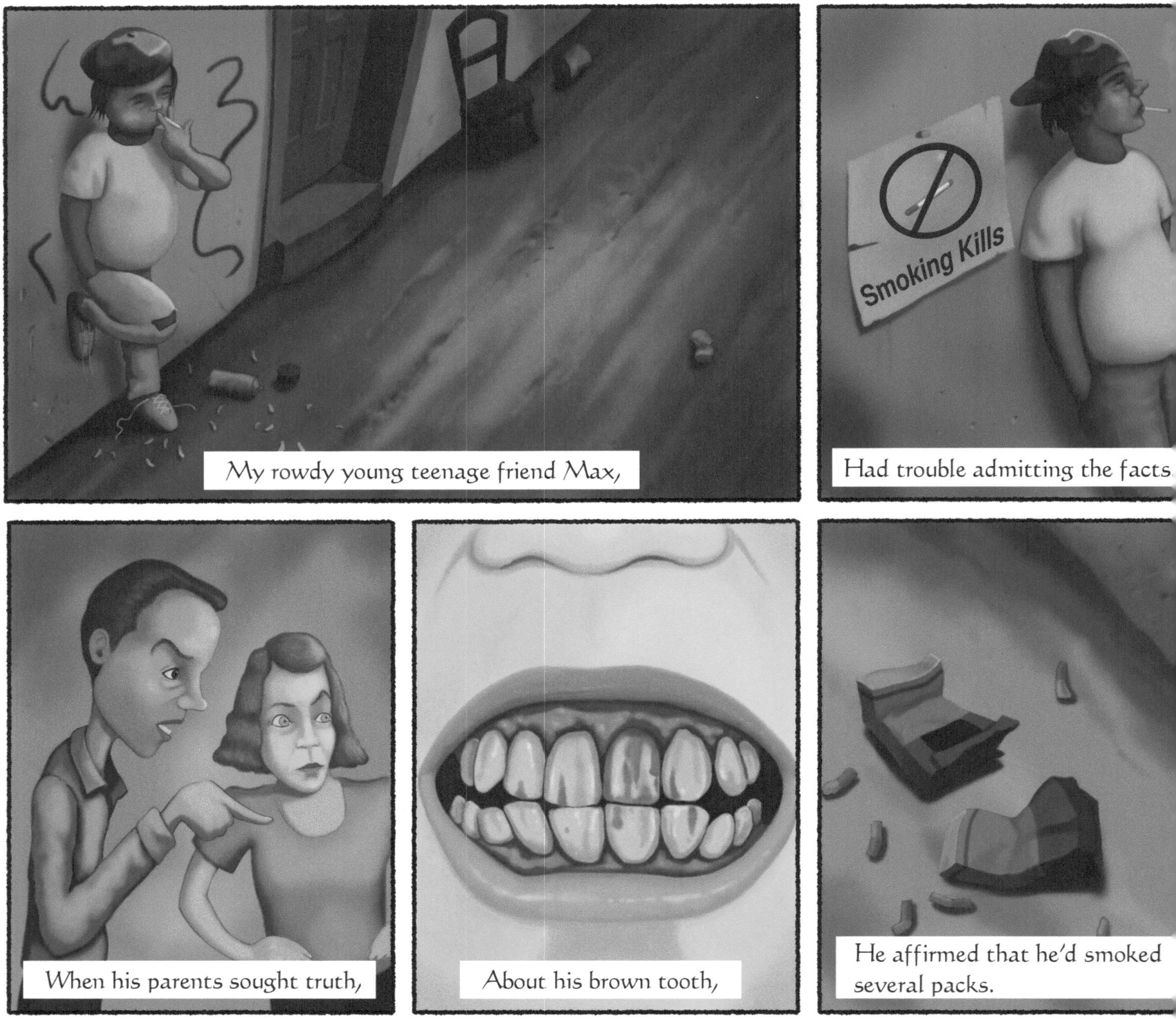
My rowdy young teenage friend Max,
Smoking Kills
Had trouble admitting the facts
When his parents sought truth,
About his brown tooth,
He affirmed that he'd smoked several packs.

Teens often begin smoking cigarettes without understanding how powerful the addicting chemical nicotine can be. Many young people don't realize that trying just one cigarette can lead to a life-long addiction. Most adult smokers began the habit in their teenage years. The addictive effects of nicotine can take hold within days. Smoking is the single greatest cause of preventable disease and death in the United States. Smoking harms every organ in the human body. Common health problems associated with smoking include heart disease, emphysema, and various cancers. Chewing tobacco, smokeless tobacco, and electronic cigarettes also pose a risk to your health. Cigarette smoke gives your clothes an unpleasant odor, causes bad breath, and yes, it also stains your teeth. Remember, if you don't start you'll never have to quit.

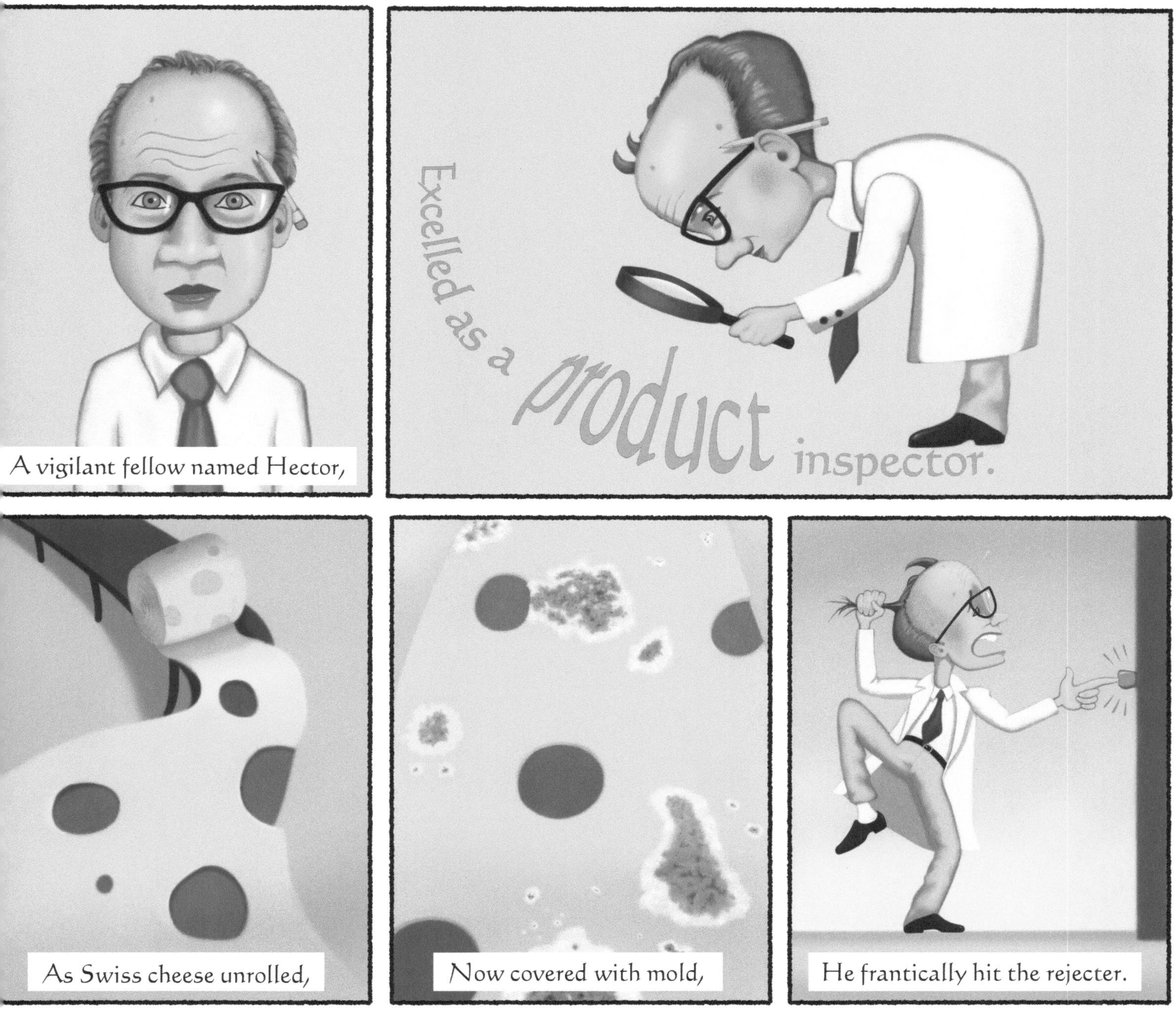
A vigilant fellow named Hector,
Excelled as a product inspector.
As Swiss cheese unrolled,
Now covered with mold,
He frantically hit the rejecter.

When you stroll down the aisles of your neighborhood grocery store, it's easy to take for granted that the food you purchase is safe to eat. Each part of the supply chain is inspected to ensure the safety of our food supply. Included are growers, manufacturers, distributors, and retail stores. Still, it's a good idea to get in the habit of reading expiration dates because some products can remain on the shelves well past the time of expiration. Since bacteria are easily transferred to and from food, always wash your hands thoroughly before and after handling food. While cooking, harmful bacteria in the juices of raw meat and poultry must not contact countertops, utensils, and dishes. Cross-contamination in the kitchen can cause severe foodborne illnesses. Rinsing fresh fruits and vegetables under running water helps to remove pesticides, bacteria, and other microbes. Finally, when in doubt, toss it out. If you suspect that food may be spoiled, play it safe and dispose of it. The health consequences are never worth the few pennies saved.

An anglerfish roamed Monterey,

So brilliantly lighting the way.

Through dark, cloudy seas,

Swam mermaids with ease,

Swim this way!

Just cruising their route through the bay.

The fascinating anglerfish is found in a dark, lightless habitat miles below the surface of the ocean. The female uses a special adaptation resembling an overhanging fishing rod to attract a tasty meal. On the end of the rod sits a glowing lure created by bioluminescent bacteria that live within the anglerfish. Bioluminescence is the same process used by fireflies. The green glow sticks used by children on Halloween employ a similar action. This glowing beacon hanging out in front of the anglerfish attracts unsuspecting prey toward the drifting creature's powerful jaws. The enormous, razor-sharp, translucent teeth are so large the anglerfish is unable to close its wide, crescent-shaped mouth!

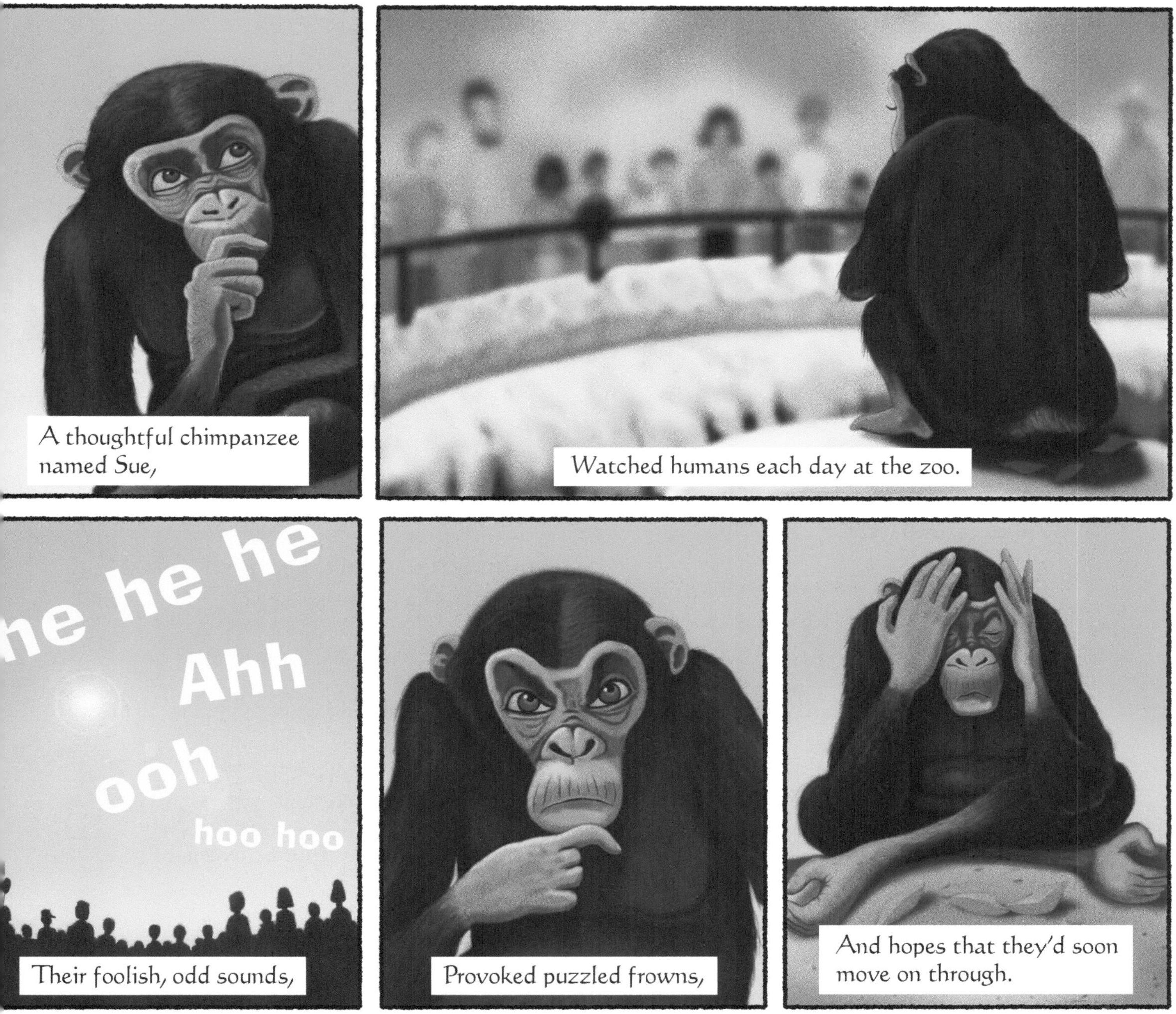
A thoughtful chimpanzee named Sue,
Watched humans each day at the zoo.
he he
Ahh
ooh
hoo hoo
Their foolish, odd sounds,
Provoked puzzled frowns,
And hopes that they'd soon move on through.

Chimpanzees are considered the closest living relative to humans because we share 98 percent of the same DNA. In 1960 researcher Jane Goodall began a long-term study living among the chimpanzees in the forests of Tanzania, in central Africa. She made the startling observation that chimpanzees use tools for more purposes than any other member of the animal kingdom. They use sticks to retrieve tasty insects from their nests, employ stones to open nuts, lace together tree branches for a comfortable bed, and skillfully use leaves as a sponge to soak up water for drinking. Chimpanzees have shown an impressive ability to learn and perform complex tasks. For instance, three months before Alan Shepard became the first American in space, Ham the Astrochimp boarded a Mercury spacecraft boosted by a Redstone rocket for a 16- minute suborbital flight, 115 miles above the earth. Ham brilliantly performed his duties pulling levers to help scientists learn critical information about the effects of weightlessness, acceleration, and the ability to work in space. Ham was a true space pioneer who paved the way for the astronauts that followed.

GLOSSARY

audacious: very confident and daring: bold

auricle: the outer part of the ear; pinna

bioluminescence: light given off naturally by certain kinds of fish, insects, or bacteria

bubonic plague: a serious disease that is spread especially by rats that killed many people during the Middle Ages

embellish: to add beauty by providing details or ornaments

emphysema: a disease in which the lungs become stretched and breathing becomes difficult

gelatinous: having the nature of or resembling jelly

ingest: to take, as food into the body

innovative: introducing or using new ideas or methods

intrepid: having no fear: very daring and bold

lavish: given in large amounts: having a very rich and expensive quality

patent: a document granting an inventor the right to be the only one that can make or sell a product for a certain number of years

notorious: well-known or famous for something bad

plunder: to steal things from a place with the use of force

pulsate: to make strong regular beats

raucous: loud and unpleasant to listen to

shtick: an often repeated theatrical or comic performance

solitary: alone without anyone or anything else

stratified: arranged or formed in layers

successive: following one another in a series without interruption

translucent: not completely clear or transparent, but clear enough to allow the passage of light

traverse: to pass or move over, along, or through

vigilant: keenly watchful and alert to trouble or danger

CPSIA information can be obtained
at www.ICGtesting.com
Printed in the USA
LVHW071009150719
624094LV00011B/244/P
* 9 7 8 1 7 3 2 8 1 8 6 0 6 *